Original title:
Cosmic Clownery

Copyright © 2025 Creative Arts Management OÜ
All rights reserved.

Author: Jasper Montgomery
ISBN HARDBACK: 978-1-80567-813-7
ISBN PAPERBACK: 978-1-80567-934-9

Starlight Shenanigans

In the night, stars dance and twirl,
Planets giggle, in spirals they swirl.
Mars juggles moons, oh what a sight,
While comets tickle the skies with delight.

Laughter echoes from Jupiter's core,
As Saturn spins rings, begging for more.
Nebulas burst into chuckles and sighs,
While space dust falls like confetti from the skies.

Whirlwinds of Witty Wonder

A twinkling star with a grin so wide,
Whirls through the cosmos, full of pride.
Black holes chuckle, pulling all near,
In a giggling vortex, it twists, oh dear!

Shooting stars race, not a moment to waste,
Chasing their tails in a cosmic haste.
Planets play hopscotch around a bright sun,
In this stellar game, everyone's having fun!

Cosmic Quips on an Interstellar Stage

A comedy show in the dark of space,
Aliens tumble, tripping when they race.
Galaxies wink from their starry seats,
As meteors crash with hilarious beats.

Asteroids throw pies across the light years,
While starlit laughter wipes away all fears.
Planets crack jokes, trading puns with flair,
In the grandest show, no one seems to care.

The Celestial Circus of Dreams

Under the moon, a ring is in place,
With comical creatures from outer space.
Acrobats float with a giggle and cheer,
While silly space bears juggle with fear.

Each act more wacky than the one before,
Gravity's rules? They simply ignore!
In this merry show, laughter's the key,
In the universe's heart, wild and free!

Silly Stars in Stardust Shadows

In the night where giggles gleam,
Silly stars begin to dream.
They juggle moons and spin in flight,
Painting laughs across the night.

Comets twirl with playful grace,
While black holes hide a smiling face.
Nebulas puff out merry sighs,
As shooting stars wear goofy ties.

Planets waltz in polka dots,
With suns that burn like boiling pots.
Each twinkle holds a cheeky grin,
Inviting all the joy within.

On stardust paths, the laughter flows,
Where every orbit spins and glows.
In this expanse, no worries dwell,
Just jests and joy that cast a spell.

Dance of the Cosmic Mirth

Underneath the glitter bright,
Jokers leap into the night.
Galaxies twist, and planets play,
In a merry, cosmic ballet.

With a wink from every sun,
They bounce and flip — oh what fun!
Asteroids catch a snicker's sound,
As laughter twirls all around.

The milky way becomes a stage,
Where every star turns a page.
Witty whispers in the air,
As gravity has lost its care.

Comet tails and laughter blend,
As every loop finds a new friend.
In this dance of joy and cheer,
The universe knows no fear.

A Whirlwind in the Milky Way

Stars twirl like dancers, no care in the night,
Their giggles echo, a wondrous delight.
Planets join in, with a wobbly spin,
Spinning through space, let the laughter begin.

Shooting stars race, chasing silly dreams,
In a cosmic circus, bursting at the seams.
Nebulas puff, like cotton candy clouds,
With every twist, they cheer out loud!

Laughter's Light Year Journey

A comet came whizzing, with a smile so bright,
Carrying joy, through the velvet night.
Wormholes giggle, with cheeky surprise,
As quasar jokes light up the skies.

Aliens chuckle, in their funky tall ships,
Trading punchlines and intergalactic quips.
Zero gravity tickles, oh what a sight,
As laughter erupts in the dark of the night!

The Cosmic Comedy of Colliding Worlds

Planets collide in a hug so absurd,
Creating a mess, yet not a single word.
Asteroids tumble in a galactic ballet,
Falling with grace, in a funny array.

Stars shake hands, with a twinkle and jest,
Creating a scene that's simply the best.
Galaxies swirling, in whimsical play,
Their laughter cascading, drifting away.

Gravitational Guffaws

Black holes chuckle, with a sneaky embrace,
Pulling in stars with a giggling grace.
Gravity teases, with its silly strings,
Sending all comets for jolly old swings.

Supernovae burst, with glittery cheer,
Exploding in colors that tickle the sphere.
In this playful realm, joy knows no bounds,
Where the universe dances to laughter's sweet sounds!

The Trapeze of Time and Space

In a twirl of glitter and glee,
A jester swings from a chandelier tree.
Balancing facts that bend and break,
Giggles resonate with each leap they take.

Spaceships painted in polka-dot hues,
Echo laughter through the vast cosmic views.
The clock ticks backward, a jest in its chime,
In this waltz with the absurd, we dance through time.

Cosmic Capers at Dusk

As the sun dips low with a playful frown,
Aliens jive in a sequined gown.
Stars wink from their celestial stage,
Join the merriment, turn the page.

Jumping comets with silly grins,
Skate on rings where the laughter spins.
Dancing mistakes in the dance of fate,
Hold on tight, it's never too late.

Revelry Among the Stars

Under a blanket of shimmering light,
Jesters tumble in the velvet night.
Galaxies whirl in a daring game,
Each one absurd, but all the same.

Nibbling on cakes made of stardust dreams,
Giggles erupt like bursting seams.
In this ballet of the strange and bright,
Laughter echoes through the cosmic night.

The Witty Wasteland of Space

On a barren plain where no one would tread,
A space clown dances with a floppy red head.
Creating mirth from the dust and the void,
In this empty expanse, joy's not destroyed.

With balloons of gas that tickle the sky,
And friendly robots who wink as they fly.
They craft a carnival, witty and sly,
In the heart of the vast where giggles never die.

Gravity's Graceful Gags

In a world where apples fly,
Stars dance, they twist and tie.
Planets tumble, with a cheer,
Laughter echoes, far and near.

Floating fish in the air,
Juggling galaxies with flair.
Asteroids roll with a grin,
In this circus, all join in.

A comet slips on a ring,
What a sight, what joy they bring!
As the black holes suck and play,
With cosmic laughs, we drift away.

Saturn's Silly Serenade

Saturn sings a tune so bright,
With ringed hats and neon light.
Its moons join in with squishy sounds,
In this space show, joy abounds.

Jumping jellies, zero G,
All the stars dance just like me.
Twinkling lights in a funny way,
Reflect the laughs of night and day.

A meteor darts with a wink,
Turning stardust into pink.
With every chuckle from afar,
Saturn shines like a superstar.

Comedic Choreography of the Cosmos

A waltz of comets, spinning round,
With cosmic beats in silence found.
Nebulae puff with a smile,
Filling the void with humor's style.

Galaxies groove, they swirl and sway,
Invisible jokes lead the way.
Planets twirl in a fancy dress,
While supernovas burst with finesse.

Gravity pranks in a cosmic play,
Pulling us all in a silly way.
Astronauts giggle as they fly,
Among the laughter of the sky.

Spacetime Acrobatics

Time loops back for a comic flip,
Stars perform on a wobbly tip.
A cosmic tightrope, thin and bright,
Where stardust spills in pure delight.

Black holes spin with dizzy grace,
Swirling stars in a playful race.
Light beams zigzag, with heart so free,
As spacetime bends in hilarity.

Falling meteors like jesters beam,
In this vast universe of dream.
Every giggle breaks the night,
Creating joy in dazzling flight.

Jovian Jest

In the vastness above, where the planets spin,
A jolly giant winks with a bubbly grin.
Saturn's rings twirl in a playful show,
While Martian mischief makes the comets glow.

A dancing star twinkles with carefree flair,
While meteors tumble like they just don't care.
Galactic giggles echo across the black,
As the nebulae shimmer in a jazzy pack.

Lunar Laughter

The moon beams down with a silvery smirk,
As shadows on Earth do a whimsical jerk.
Crickets start chirping a comical tune,
Beneath the light of a jovial moon.

A bunny on Mars hops in a silly way,
As the stars wink back, encouraging play.
Laughs are contagious in the pale moonlight,
Where everyone joins in the magical night.

The Clown's Starlit Voyage

A spaceship sails with a whoopee cushion,
Through galaxies bright, causing a commotion.
With every blast and a gleeful sound,
Space travelers giggle as antics abound.

The captain juggles with stars in a dance,
While asteroids swirl as if caught in a trance.
With a thud and a bump, they spin out of line,
All of the cosmos is theirs to define.

Cosmic Hijinks Among the Stars

Between twinkling stars, where the wild things play,
Galaxies giggle, swirling bright and gay.
A supernova bursts in a sparkly cheer,
While Jupiter chuckles at the fun far and near.

With each cosmic tumble through this vast domain,
Planets erupt with a hilarious strain.
Shooting stars race to a laugh-out-loud beat,
As the universe grooves on delightfully sweet.

Antics of the Astral Buffoons

In space where the wild jesters make their home,
The asteroids grin as they twirl and roam.
Galactic jesters juggle with comets that hiss,
Creating a ruckus, not one star can miss.

With playful pokes, they spring and they leap,
In the fabric of night, their laughter runs deep.
Nebulas roll with glee at the sight,
Of astral buffoons causing joy in the night.

Winks from the Universe

Twinkling lights in the night sky,
Whispers of fun as they fly by.
A dancing comet, a silly spree,
The universe grins, so wild and free.

In velvet black with a gleeful twist,
Planets chuckle, they can't resist.
Galaxies spin in a playful race,
Sending joy through the vast space.

Jesters Among Stars

The moon wears a hat, oh what a sight,
Shooting stars play tag through the night.
With twirls and flips, they make a fuss,
An interstellar circus, just for us.

Planets juggle their orbiting moons,
While meteors dance to lively tunes.
A cosmic comedy, unfurling wide,
Oh, how they laugh, on this galactic ride.

Eclipsed Faces and Laughing Stars

When shadows play hide and seek,
The sun and moon share a wink so sleek.
Stars peek out from behind their veils,
Giggling softly at forgotten tales.

Light years away, the echoes ring,
Cosmic chuckles, the darkness sings.
In this realm where joy ignites,
Every hidden face brings sheer delights.

Gravity's Goofballs

Floating far, the antics abound,
Silly asteroids rolling around.
With each bump and bungle in their play,
They trip through space, what a display!

Black holes chuckle, their swirl so wide,
While comets giggle, in stellar glide.
Gravity's jest, a whimsical dance,
In this grand show, we all take a chance.

The Galaxy's Giggle Festival

Stars wink in playful delight,
Planets jive with cosmic light.
Comets streak with silly smiles,
And laughter dances for miles.

Nebulas puff and puff,
Creating clouds of fluffy stuff.
Black holes swirl in merry spins,
As joy erupts where laughter begins.

Asteroids bounce like bouncy balls,
Rockets zoom through cosmic halls.
The sun beamed down a cheerful glow,
While aliens put on quite a show.

In this festival of glee,
Universe full of jubilee.
Let the giggles take their flight,
And revel all through the night.

The Laughs that Echo in the Void

Whispers tickle the empty space,
As echoes dance in a joyous race.
Stars chuckle with twinkling eyes,
While silence sings of sweet surprise.

Floating jokes from comet trails,
Spread the laughter in cosmic gales.
Galaxies wobble with pure glee,
In the vastness, hilarity is free.

Astrological puns collide,
As planets spin in giggling stride.
A wink from Venus, a grin from Mars,
Together they burst like shooting stars.

Through the void, the chuckles soar,
Each jest a key to unlock more.
In the universe, joy prevails,
As laughter sails on cosmic trails.

Wormholes of Wit

Through portals of silliness we slide,
Where laughter and joy collide.
Whirling in a zany race,
Sprinkling chuckles across the space.

Wormholes twist with witty surprise,
As clever quips explode and rise.
Every turn a new delight,
In these tunnels, joy takes flight.

Punchlines echo, never cease,
In this realm, humor is peace.
Quarks and quirks chase each other,
In a symphony of giggles, they shudder.

Gravitational pulls of jest,
Bouncing beams, never at rest.
Wormholes glowing with laughter bright,
Lead us all to the endless night!

The Celestial Circus

In the ring of the starry sky,
A circus plays, oh me, oh my!
Planets juggle with rings so grand,
While meteors leap at their command.

Galactic clowns in vibrant gear,
With cosmic antics that draw near.
Orbiting moons twirl and glide,
With a silly bounce, they take off wide.

Shooting stars shoot through the joy,
Each a bright explosion, oh boy!
The Milky Way becomes a stage,
As laughter bursts in every age.

Time stands still in this wild dance,
In the universe, joy has a chance.
Step right up, join the fray,
In this celestial circus, play!

Astronomical Amusement

In the sky, a jester flies,
With stars that twinkle, brighter lies.
He juggles planets, round and round,
While comets giggle, making sound.

Galaxies swirl in silly dance,
As meteors leap, they take a chance.
Black holes snicker, pulling near,
A joyride through the cosmic sphere.

Nebulas puff in rainbow hues,
Tickling space with vibrant views.
Gravity pulls, but laughter stays,
In this whimsical, starry maze.

With each blast of a supernova,
The universe plans its next bigova.
So chuckle with the stars tonight,
In the vastness, all feels right.

The Comic Constellation

Stars align in a cheeky grin,
As constellations dance, spin and spin.
Orion trips on his own bright belt,
Sagittarius winks, a joke is dealt.

The Little Dipper spills some light,
While the Big Dipper takes flight.
Planets laugh in playful rows,
Echoing joy, the cosmos knows.

A shooting star does flips and spins,
While Venus giggles, divine grins.
Uranus chuckles with a blue hue,
Tickled by the laughter anew.

Comets wear hats in absurd styles,
Tickling space with their bright smiles.
So gaze at the heavens, take your shot,
Find humor in the vast and forgot.

Laughter Etched in Stardust

In the void, a chuckle rings,
As stardust wraps forgotten things.
Each twinkle holds a secret joke,
Disguised in silence, softly spoke.

Astronauts float with a silly face,
Playing tag in zero gravity space.
A burst of giggles, and they collide,
Stars erupt as they confide.

Saturn's rings laugh in delight,
While Mercury zooms in a flash of light.
Galactic jokes, so bizarre and sweet,
Turn black holes into comedic feats.

Eclipses wink, a playful game,
Cosmic silliness, never the same.
So let the universe bring you cheer,
Stardust giggles are always near.

The Multi-Dimensional Stage Show

On a stage that's round and vast,
Dimensions shift, the die is cast.
Time plays tricks, and space is bent,
Laughter flows, pure and unspent.

Planets perform in dazzling hues,
With each act, they share their news.
A comet sings, a black hole hums,
The audience claps as time succumbs.

Wormholes whirl, a dizzying ride,
As humor sails the cosmic tide.
Galactic acrobats fly and dive,
In this stage, how they thrive!

Dimensions giggle, like a child,
Transforming space, so absurd and wild.
Witness the spectacle way up high,
In this grand show, let laughter sigh.

The Silly Symphony of Satellites

In the sky where comets dance,
The satellites play a silly trance.
Jupiter jumps and Mars twirls around,
As giggles of moons make a joyful sound.

Stars wear hats made of rainbow hue,
Chasing each other in a playful queue.
Each twinkle's a note in a cosmic song,
Together they hum, all night long.

Nebulas spin like a grand showgirl,
Revealing secrets in a swirling whirl.
Asteroids chuckle, bumping in glee,
While space dust sparkles, wild and free.

In this realm where laughter reigns,
The universe jests, shedding all chains.
So close your eyes and dream of the night,
Where the heavens giggle with pure delight.

Stardust Shenanigans

In a nebula's heart, where colors collide,
Stardust sprinkles like confetti in stride.
Planets parade in a comical race,
Rockets laugh as they zoom into space.

Moons on unicycles wobbly ride,
Winking at asteroids, full of pride.
Twinkling stars play hide and seek,
As laughter echoes from meek to sleek.

Galaxies swirl with cheeky grins,
Spinning tales of their silly sins.
Cosmic jesters flip and they fly,
While comets race with a wink of an eye.

Floating through laughter in a star-lit trend,
Every moment in space, a joke without end.
Join in the fun, let your spirit roam,
In this universe, you always feel home.

Mirrored Galaxies and Goofy Grins

Two galaxies mirror in a goofy dance,
Twinkling stars caught in a cosmic trance.
They tease and spin in a radiant whirl,
As supernovas burst with a joyful twirl.

Planets poke fun at their sibling's size,
While black holes chuckle at the vacuum's lies.
In every corner, there's laughter to find,
A universe bursting with humor entwined.

Comedic comets streak past with ease,
Turning the night air into cosmic tease.
With every supernova, a grin they share,
Joy spreads through space, floating in the air.

So gather round, let your chuckles resound,
In this quirky expanse, laughter's profound.
Embrace the absurd; let silliness spin,
For even the stars wear their goofy grins.

Interstellar Laugh Lines

Through the void, where the giggles burst,
Interstellar pranksters quench the thirst.
They spin jokes on solar winds so free,
While meteors tumble with glee and esprit.

Each quasar a quip, bright as a flame,
Stars wink, knowing they're all part of the game.
The universe sways, full of playful jest,
In the fabric of space, humor knows no rest.

Comets carve smiles in the darkened skies,
With mischievous tales that make spirits rise.
Shooting stars slide by with charming flair,
As laughter erupts in a magical air.

So ride the waves of this cheerful spree,
Let the cosmos twinkle with whimsy and glee.
In the dance of the heavens, embrace the fight,
For every laugh line draws in pure delight.

Jokes that Light the Dark

In the void where shadows play,
A laughter echoes through the gray.
Planets spin, they dance with glee,
As comets wink, just wait and see.

Galaxies twirl in silly socks,
While space-time puns come in clusters of blocks.
Stars shoot jokes that tickle the night,
With a punchline bright enough to ignite.

Asteroids roll like laughing stones,
Tickling moons with cosmic tones.
Laughter bursts like neon rays,
Lighting up the dark's funny ways.

So gather round, in joy we dwell,
In the universe's punch-drunk spell.
For in the dark, humor is key,
To unlock the stars' great jubilee.

A Dance of Stars and Snickers

In the ballet of the endless skies,
Stars shuffle their feet, oh what a surprise!
With twinkling eyes, they break into cheer,
As laughter from worlds spins far and near.

Galactic waltz with a twisty beat,
Planets pirouette on a meteoric street.
Nebulas giggle, bursting in hue,
While stardust confetti spirals anew.

Shooting stars hurl jests so bold,
Tickling the darkness, a sight to behold.
In this dance where the comets glide,
Humor and joy take cosmic pride.

So spin and twirl in the starry dome,
Where jokes and jigs take flight from home.
For in the rhythm of all that gleams,
Laughter flows like magical streams.

Intergalactic Jesters

On a galactic stage, jesters leap,
With oversized shoes, they give laughs a sweep.
A wink from the sun, a nudge from the moon,
Creating a dance that makes all hearts swoon.

Wormholes stretch with a giggly curl,
As laughter whirls in a cosmic swirl.
Black holes snicker, pulling in light,
While stars tease comets in playful flight.

Dressed in the colors of distant dust,
Space-folk chuckle, it's a must!
With every quip, they bump and grind,
Leaving joy in the universe behind.

So raise up a toast to the cosmic jest,
Where humor reigns and hearts are blessed.
In the void where laughter sparks,
The interstellar play ignites the dark.

Celestial Fool's Odyssey

Across the skies where jesters roam,
Planetary pranksters make space their home.
With magical tricks that defy all norms,
They cause the stars to dance in forms.

A comet slips on a cosmic ice,
Making the universe giggle, oh so nice.
Saturn spins in rings of laugh,
As galaxies share their jovial craft.

Every nova bursts with a chuckle bright,
Even the dark matter feels the light.
In the fabric of space, humor entwined,
With every joke, a new star aligned.

Through time and space, their antics are grand,
Laughter lingers with a gentle hand.
For in the cosmos, joy is the key,
To a fool's odyssey, wild and free.

The Gravity-Defying Fool

In space he juggles moonbeams bright,
Tumbling stars in sheer delight.
With a wink he flips the comet's tail,
And all the galaxies cheer and hail.

He wears a hat of shimmering light,
Dancing through the blackened night.
His laughter twinkles, a joyful sound,
As he bounces where the wild stars abound.

Around his feet, the asteroids roll,
He giggles as they take a stroll.
Gravity's rules, he does defy,
In the grand stage of the velvet sky.

With a pirouette, he takes a leap,
In the void, he twirls, no time for sleep.
The universe grins at his silly spree,
A dazzling jester, forever free.

Playful Planets in Pantomime

Round and round, the planets play,
In a lovely, silly ballet.
Mars wears a giant polka-dot suit,
While Venus dances to the cosmic flute.

Jupiter jumps with a thunderous clap,
While Saturn spins in a dazzling gap.
Neptune giggles, a cascade of glee,
As they twirl beneath a starry marquee.

The sun beams brightly, a spotlight bright,
Illuminating their whimsical flight.
A cosmic stage where laughter flows,
Every moment, a new joke that glows.

With a wink, they wink, the planets shout,
In their celestial play, laughter's about.
Oh, what a scene, a merry mirth,
In this universe, a joyful birth!

Cosmic Chuckles Through the Cosmos

At the edge of the bright Milky Way,
A ticklish ghost likes to play.
Filling comets with a giggling breeze,
Making the constellations freeze.

Shooting stars race, led by their glee,
As they tickle the depths of infinity.
A laughter echo in the silent void,
With each burst of joy, worries destroyed.

Asteroids roll with a raucous cheer,
Spreading giggles to planets far and near.
A mirthful echo through space and time,
Each chuckle a note, a whimsical rhyme.

In this grand expanse, where silence swells,
Joyous sparkles weave tales and spells.
For laughter knows no bounds in this sphere,
Around every corner, it lingers near.

The Amusing Archives of Andromeda

In Andromeda, stories unfold,
Of silly stardust, bright and bold.
Puppets of light in a comic play,
Whirling through time in their own ballet.

Each twinkling star holds a tale to tell,
Of playful antics where laughter fell.
A giggle in the black, a chuckle in the blue,
With each passing comet, something new.

The echoes of laughter stretch far and wide,
As shooting stars take a joyful ride.
In the archives of humor, forever they beam,
Creating a universe where joy reigns supreme.

Every twist and spin, a laugh in disguise,
Through the void, a symphony of bright smiles.
In this galactic vault, fun never lacks,
With memories of joy that the cosmos tracks.

The Comet's Playful Grin

In the sky, a bright tail sways,
An artist drawing silly rays.
With stardust paints, it weaves delight,
A playful grin in the cosmic night.

Planets giggle as they twirl,
While moons bounce like a playful pearl.
Each twinkling star shares a joke,
As comets dance and stars provoke.

A meteor zips and makes a fuss,
While shooting stars burst forth with lust.
They whisper jokes of lightyears long,
In this vast stage where they belong.

Laughter echoes through the void,
In orbits round, none are devoid.
The universe spins with cheeky cheer,
As the comet's grin draws all near.

Galaxies in Guffaws

Spirals twist with laughter wide,
In the dance, all stars abide.
Supernovae burst with glee,
A glowing show, so wild and free.

Black holes chuckle, deep and sly,
As planets whirl and swing on by.
Each star a joke, a witty spark,
In swirling lanes, igniting the dark.

Nebulas puff with cosmic jest,
Crafting colors at their best.
With playful puffs, they tease the light,
Encircling worlds in sheer delight.

Gravity tugs with gentle hands,
Twinkling dust across the lands.
Galaxies giggle, bright with pride,
In this vast show, we all reside.

Interstellar Harlequins

The planets wear polka dots and stripes,
Juggling moons with giggling gripes.
Each wink and twirl, a grand affair,
In the vastness, joy is everywhere.

Meteor jesters leap and bound,
With twirls and flips, they astound.
They land with chuckles, oh so spry,
Tickling the comets racing by.

Quasars wink from far-off skies,
Their beams of laughter light our eyes.
Dancing in circuits, they sway so bold,
A cosmic circus, fun to behold.

With starlit pies and nebula pies,
The universe laughs, bright and wise.
Interstellar tricks and playful spins,
In this grand realm, joy always wins.

The Universe's Witty Masquerade

Stars don bright masks of dazzling hue,
Each one gleeful, a lively crew.
Winking planets in splendid display,
In the galaxy's grand ballet.

Galactic jesters twirl and play,
In the spotlight of a sunlit ray.
With whispers of comets from afar,
Each act ignites the night's bizarre.

Whirling asteroids spin in glee,
Creating a ruckus, wild and free.
Saturn's rings clink like pots and pans,
While laughter echoes in distant lands.

Bright novas giggle, explode with flair,
Sprinkling joy through the thinning air.
In cosmic chaos, smiles parade,
As the universe, oh, what a charade!

The Eclipsed Performer's Dream

In the darkness of the night,
A jester lost his way,
He tripped on moonbeams bright,
And laughed at stars' ballet.

Galaxies spun in a swirl,
His big shoes squeaked in glee,
A tumble, a cartwheel, a twirl,
He danced with a comet's spree.

Planets chuckled, rings did shake,
As meteors formed a band,
Their raucous tunes made him wake,
In laughter, he took a stand.

With each giggle from the sky,
He juggled words in air,
For even when stars sigh,
They join in whimsical flair.

Saturn's Ringmaster Revels

Saturn donned a bright top hat,
With moons as audience small,
He cracked jokes, oh what of that!
His rings began to sprawl.

A cosmic circus in the night,
A shooting star flew past,
Acrobats of sheer delight,
In the vastness, they amassed.

He tossed a ball made of dust,
And planets chimed along,
In laughter's twinkling thrust,
They sang an astral song.

Nebulas swirled in bright hues,
Tickling asteroids that spun,
The ringmaster laughed at their views,
A show that's never done.

Asteroids and Absurdities

Asteroids rolled in joyful jest,
Bouncing off the Milky Way,
In costumes that they wore best,
They frolicked on their play.

Selves dressed in cosmic thread,
They spun a tale of cheer,
With every tumble as they sped,
They whispered secrets dear.

A lollipop star shone so bright,
As they danced in wacky glee,
While shooting stars took flight,
Like confetti, wild and free.

In the vast expanse they played,
Jester hats on little rocks,
With giggles, their paths they laid,
Creating cosmic knocks.

Whimsical Whirls in the Void

In the void where silence sighs,
Whirls of color start to tease,
A funny face in endless skies,
Inviting all to see.

With a bounce, a joyful twist,
Galaxies peeked to play,
The stars chuckled, none could resist,
In their cosmic ballet.

Planets formed a conga line,
Swinging to the cosmic beat,
In perfect jest, they felt divine,
Naught but joy, oh how sweet!

In the laughter of the spheres,
Absurdities take flight,
For in the depths of cosmic cheers,
All is silly delight.

Stars in Painted Faces

Twinkling lights in a silly game,
Winking down with a playful flame.
Each one dressed in shades so bright,
Chasing shadows throughout the night.

Galaxies giggle in a merry spin,
As planets spin tales of where they've been.
Jovial sprites dance on Mars's dust,
Creating chaos; it's a must!

Comets carry pies, oh what a sight,
Whipping through space in a dizzy flight.
Stars trumpet laughter with radiant beams,
Scattering joy like vivid dreams.

In this realm where the jesters thrive,
A cosmic circus keeps dreams alive.
Each spark a cheeky wink from afar,
A reminder to smile, wherever you are.

The Galaxy's Prankster Dance

In the Milky Way, jesters abound,
Spinning and twirling upon the ground.
Galactic giggles echo so wide,
As mischief rides on a comet's glide.

Saturn's rings wear hats and bows,
While meteors paint the skies with shows.
Each black hole a stage for ludic laughs,
Where stardust twirls and the universe chaffs.

Dark matter plays hide and seek,
With bright suns shining their playful peek.
All while the moons just roll and cheer,
Celebrating fun, year after year.

From Andromeda's side to Orion's heart,
Every joke is a cosmic work of art.
So let the universe dance and prance,
In the swirling skies, we join the dance.

Nebulae and Nonsense

Fluffy clouds puff out a giggle or two,
Painting the cosmos in a bright hue.
Catch the jokes in the swirling mist,
Where stars and omens happily twist.

Jokes fly on solar winds so sweet,
Tickling asteroids as they compete.
A meteor shower of chuckles galore,
As laughter echoes on the cosmic floor.

Whimsical wonders float through the void,
Each colorful flash a smile deployed.
Nebulae wrap tales in ribbons of light,
Whispering secrets of the joyous night.

In this universe of jests and glee,
Every twinkle holds a chuckle, it's true.
So join the fun in this celestial spree,
And celebrate magic, wild and free.

Laughter Beyond the Moons

In the shadows where the starlight streams,
Lies a carnival of whimsical dreams.
Each moon a joker, grinning wide,
With merry prancing across the tide.

Under the glow of a radiant sun,
Planets spin tales of joy and fun.
Galaxies burst into fits of delight,
As laughter twinkles in the serene night.

Space is a playground, cosmic and vast,
Where every moment is built to last.
Silly songs float on gravity's pull,
As the universe revels, beautifully full.

So let every star twinkle and shine,
With echoes of laughter in the grand design.
In this comedic dance of the endless skies,
We find joy painted in our eyes.

Orbiting Chuckles

In the dance of stars, they glide and spin,
Silly shadows playing, where laughter begins.
Galaxies twirl in a jovial chase,
Tickling the void with a bright, goofy face.

Planets parade with their wobbly hats,
Juggling comets like playful acrobats.
With giggles that echo through endless expanse,
The universe chuckles in a cosmic dance.

Meteor showers rain down with glee,
As stardust forms prisms of whimsy, you see.
Twinkling spectacles on this celestial stage,
While the cosmos beams with laughter, no age.

But when black holes yawn, oh, what a sight!
Swallowing light, but all feels just right.
For in these mysteries, the humor's profound,
In the orbit of chuckles, joy spins round.

Quasar Quips and Tricks

A quasar sparkles with mischievous flair,
Winking at starlight that dances in air.
They send out jokes in bursts of bright light,
And cosmic giggles echo throughout the night.

In the heart of the void, where silence might reign,
Laughter erupts like a funny chain.
Each punchline delivered from far, distant lands,
Gathers the stardust like magical bands.

Space dust tickles the cheek of a moon,
As it spins in rhythm to a whimsical tune.
Jokes weaved in gravity, stretching the fun,
In the tapestry woven by stars 'til it's done.

Lightyears apart but they all join in,
With puns that ignite like rockets in spin.
The universe stifles a chuckle so loud,
Oh, the quasar's tricks make the galaxies proud!

Pranks of the Pulsars

Pulsars are pranksters, tickling the vast,
With beams of bright laughter, a light-hearted blast.
From rhythm to rhythm, they play their sweet game,
Sending cosmic smirks, no two stars the same.

With each marked beat, the universe grins,
As pulsar jokes echo where silence begins.
They bounce off black holes like playful little spheres,
And the night sky erupts into joyful cheers.

Galactic jesters with twinkling delight,
Whispering whimsy in the depths of the night.
They pull on our hearts with their silly old spins,
Launching roars of laughter where life truly begins.

So bring on the humor, the stars love to play,
In the cosmic expanse, where we drift and sway.
Pranks of the pulsars, the dance of the skies,
Unleashing the chuckles that light up our eyes.

The Laughing Celestials

The celestials chuckle from every great height,
As they spin through the cosmos, a fanciful sight.
They trade silly stories, each twist full of jest,
In the warmth of their laughter, we all feel so blessed.

From fiery suns that sway in delight,
To twirling moons that flicker at night.
Each star is a player on this grand stage,
Where joy is the script and love is the rage.

Asteroids tumble, their giggles untamed,
Crashing through silence, their humor unframed.
Creating new worlds with their clarity bright,
In the laughter of celestials, they share pure light.

As we gaze at the night, we can't help but laugh,
For the universe's humor is our cosmic path.
With every twinkle, let your spirit take flight,
In the arms of the stars, where all feels just right.

Whirling Dervishes of Delight

Spinning through the stars so bright,
Laughter echoes in the night.
Twinkle toes in space they twirl,
Galactic giggles make them whirl.

Planets bounce like playful sprites,
Juggling beams of starry lights.
Comets sway in joyful jest,
In this dance, they feel the best.

Cosmic capers take their flight,
Asteroids in playful plight.
Every orbit shares a grin,
As the universe spins within.

Bouncing balls of gas and glow,
Who knew space could steal the show?
In a frame of endless cheer,
Laughter's echo reaches near.

The Milky Way's Mischief

Starry pranks in a celestial lane,
Twinkling eyes that tease and feign.
Galaxies giggle, clusters play,
Echoes of joy in a frolicsome way.

Wormholes weave their silly tricks,
Time slips by with comical kicks.
Supernovae burst in delight,
Showering chuckles through the night.

Nebulas puff with playful pouts,
As bright comets race about.
Spinning tales in stellar breezes,
Where each wink sparks laughter's sneezes.

Laughter ripples through the skies,
In every wink, a surprise lies.
Oh, the wonders of the spray,
In the Milky Way's fun play!

Entropy's Elysium of Humor

Chaos reigns with a cheeky grin,
Stars collide, and then they spin.
In this mess, the jests abound,
Uncertainty is comedic ground.

Particles dance in playful disarray,
As galaxies twirl in a merry ballet.
Laughter bursts from every place,
In the cosmic game of the human race.

Gravitational giggles pull us near,
Waves of mischief we hold dear.
In random arcs, we find our call,
As humor weaves through the cosmic wall.

In every quirk of time and space,
Wonders light up with a smiling face.
Embrace the chaos, let it be,
In entropy's realm, we're always free.

Jesters of the Infinite Night

In the void, they play their tricks,
Moonbeams hide while starlight kicks.
Jesters roam the endless dark,
Each giggle leaves a shining spark.

Shooting stars with silly names,
Bounce through twilight, dance like flames.
With every wink, they pull a stunt,
In the night, they'll always hunt.

Galactic jests with comets as pals,
Echoing laughter from cosmic halls.
In every shadow, joy ignites,
Among the jesters of the nights.

Whirling in a timeless play,
Bringing cheer, come what may.
In the infinite's embrace so tight,
Laughter swirls through the endless night.

Celestial Jester's Whimsy

Up in the sky, a jester prances,
Twinkling lights in silly dances.
Planets spin with playful cheer,
As comets giggle, bright and clear.

Shooting stars with witty lines,
Whispering secrets of cosmic signs.
Galaxies swirl in a merry swirl,
In this vast space, laughter unfurls.

Nebulae toss their colorful hats,
While solar flares play with cats.
The universe sighs, with a hearty roar,
What a show! Let's ask for more!

With stardust tickles, dreams take flight,
In the grand circus of endless night.
Behold the wonders, the jester knows,
In the ballet of stars, hilarity flows.

Starry Satire in the Void

In the vast dark, a wink appears,
A comet jokes, shifting gears.
Black holes giggle, oh what a sight,
As stardust clowns dance in the night.

Satellites snicker with satellite friends,
Orbiting laughter that never ends.
A rogue asteroid begins to prance,
While craters hum a silly dance.

Galactic gags fly through the air,
Stars poke fun with a cosmic flare.
And in this humor, all is bright,
Welcome to the starry delight!

So chuckle with me, don't be shy,
As laughter tumbles from the sky.
In this universe, joy's the trend,
A cosmic jest, around every bend.

Laughter Among the Nebulas

Amidst the swirls of color so grand,
Silly whispers from a far-off land.
Nebulas chuckle, in hues so bright,
Creating giggles in the dead of night.

Stars play tag, in brilliant displays,
Practicing antics in whimsical ways.
The universe spins with joy and jest,
In this realm, laughter's the best.

Pulsars blink with comical charm,
Winking at moons that raise alarms.
Black holes hoot as they devour,
Galactic gigs in an endless hour.

With every twinkle, the joy expands,
In cosmic cheer, let's make our plans.
For in the depths of the cosmic sea,
A universe of laughter waits for thee.

Jokes from Beyond the Stars

From the depths of space, a punchline flies,
As planets roll their goofy eyes.
Supernova's a blast, literally so,
In the heart of stars, the jokes overflow.

A quasar beams its witty flair,
While meteors whisper, "Float if you dare!"
With every twinkle, a story unfolds,
Of cosmic capers and laughter bold.

Rocket ships zoom with a honk and a laugh,
As asteroids dance, a comical craft.
Galaxies giggle in swirling delight,
In this cosmic circus, all feels right.

So gather 'round, let's share the cheer,
In this boundless void, joy is near.
With every joke from beyond the sun,
In the dance of the stars, we all have fun!

Laughter in the Infinite Abyss

In the depths where stars do twinkle,
A jester spins in silence, a sprinkle.
With a moonbeam hat and comet shoes,
They dance among the cosmic blues.

Time wobbles as they juggle light,
Each shard a joke, a playful sight.
Watch the black holes laugh and whirl,
As galaxies giggle, in a cosmic swirl.

Asteroids toss confetti around,
Creating chaos without a sound.
The universe cracks up with glee,
At the nonsense of infinity.

So let the supernovas explode,
While the clown on a nebula rode.
In the endless void so vast and deep,
Laughter echoes, never to sleep.

Gags of the Galactic Circus

Stars in stripes twirl with flair,
Ringmasters floating, suspending air.
A comet's tail is a juggling ball,
While moons do flips, having a ball.

The Martian mimes with playful sneers,
As they tickle Saturn's ringed spheres.
Galactic goats on stilts so tall,
Strutting their stuff, having a ball.

Nebulas burst with vibrant cheer,
The crowd of planets draws near.
A cosmic elephant blows a horn,
As starlight dances, never worn.

With laughter echoing through the void,
In this circus, worries are destroyed.
They tumble through suns, and shadows tease,
In this galactic dance, we find ease.

The Stellar Satirical Show

A star shines bright with a wink and grin,
It tells the jokes that make you spin.
Planets giggle, and comets sigh,
Amidst the laughter that fills the sky.

The show unfolds with a starry jest,
Each twinkle a punchline, at best.
Black holes suck in sighs of glee,
As light beams come to playfully flee.

Witty aliens take the stage,
With quirky quips that never age.
They flip through realms, in jest they weave,
A tapestry of fun, it's hard to believe.

So sit back, float on cosmic streams,
Join this playground of amusing dreams.
For in the depths of night's wide expanse,
Laughter echoes; it's the grandest dance.

Planetary Pranks and Cosmic Capers

In orbits smooth and winding trails,
Aliens play with silly gales.
Saturn's rings are the joker's hat,
While rockets zoom, and space cats spat.

A moon sneezes, causing a quake,
The asteroids giggle, for goodness' sake!
Watch Jupiter juggle its swirling storms,
As laughter is born in playful forms.

Stars trade whispers of cheeky tricks,
As supernovae erupt in flicks.
The universe plots its laughter free,
In the dance of galaxies, joy's decree.

So come one, come all to this cosmic spree,
Where humor blends with mystery.
In the grand stage of the endless night,
Pranks abound in the starlit light.

Cosmic Musings and Mischief

In the galaxy's belly, a jester swings,
With moon pies and laughter, oh the joy it brings!
Stars wink their eyes, in a playful tease,
While comets do pirouettes, dancing with ease.

Wormholes are tunnels for giggles and fun,
As spacetime does fold, oh what a run!
Black holes are vacuums for crumbs of delight,
As laughter echoes through the endless night.

Galactic balloons float, with colors so bright,
Tickling the planets in a cosmic light.
Rocket ships spiral, like tops in a spin,
While spacemen in tutus cavort with a grin.

So grab your funny glasses, let's soar in delight,
With quirks of the universe lighting the night!
Jesters of stardust, we're never alone,
In this vast, silly circus we call our home.

The Silly Space Odyssey

Through rings of Saturn, the laughter flows,
With giggly asteroids in rainbow clothes.
Planets play tag in a stellar race,
While meteors chase with a comical pace.

Dancing in orbit, the stars take a spin,
As cosmic merchants sell smiles with a grin.
Jupiter hops in a polka-dot suit,
While Neptune and Venus do a two-step hoot!

Black holes with chuckles pull everything in,
Even the punchlines are drawn with a grin.
With spaghetti and stars in a bouncy ballet,
This odyssey tickles every light-year away.

So strap on your helmets, let's twirl through the void,
In this circus of planets where chaos is joyed.
With each solar chuckle, we'll float and we'll leap,
In a universe jolly, where laughter runs deep.

Nebulous Nonsense

In a cloak of stardust, the jesters reside,
With marshmallow moons in a cosmic slide.
Witty whirlwinds tickle the space-suited crew,
While twinkling lights burst with every cue.

Galaxies giggle with mischief galore,
As space-fairies dance on the nebula floor.
Asteroids chuckle, their journey a game,
With comet jokes lighting up the cosmic fame.

Puppets of plasma perform with a cheer,
Launching balloon rockets that bubble with beer.
Each twinkling star plays a pranking role,
In this fabulous feast for the cosmic soul.

So ride on a meteor, bounce like a clown,
In the cosmos of nonsense, you'll never frown.
With laughter as fuel, we'll soar and we'll twist,
In a starry amusement where fun can't be missed.

Paradoxical Star Jumpers

Jumping through timelines, oh what a sight,
Reverse and rewind in delightfully bright.
Time loops in hula hoops, giggles all around,
As paradox plays in its whimsical sound.

With stars on springs and orbits that spin,
Every leap's an adventure, so don't you give in!
Backwards in pleasure, the laughter ignites,
Through a kaleidoscope of cosmic delights.

Jesters in spacesuits play tag with the sun,
As gravity bends for a mischievous run.
Quarks dance on rainbows, in quantum ballet,
Creating sweet laughter wherever we play.

So leap through the galaxies, dance with the fate,
In a universe where funny is never too late.
Paradoxical jumpers, let's twist and we'll shout,
In this wild cosmic circus, there's never a doubt.

Celestial Laugh Factory

In the factory of stars, laughter beams,
Jokes wrapped in comets, born from dreams.
Galactic giggles in a spiraled dance,
Twinkling humor in a star's quick glance.

Planets spin in jest, never quite still,
Jovial orbits, all wrapped in goodwill.
Meteor jesters, zipping so fast,
In this bright cosmos, fun's never past.

Laughter erupts near the rings of the night,
Bubbles of joy pop, oh what a sight!
Saturn's smiles beam down with delight,
While Uranus chuckles at our silly plight.

The Milky Way's lanes host a grand show,
With shooting stars putting on a glow.
Intergalactic pranks, laughter's delight,
In the vastness of space, everything's bright!

Ringmaster of the Universe

In the big top of space, the ringmaster smiles,
With cosmic humor that spans countless miles.
Stars in top hats toss stardust in jest,
As asteroids leap from the quasar's crest.

Galaxies spin in a vibrant parade,
While cosmic ponies put on quite a charade.
The universe teeters, a dance on a wire,
As supernovae bloom like flames that inspire.

The audience, planets, all cheer in delight,
As the cosmic ringmaster shines ever bright.
Black holes do backflips, the crowd holds their breath,
In this stellar circus, it's never a death!

Laughter's the ticket, each joke's a thrill,
In the center of orbits, we feel the chill.
A comet rides in on a rainbow slick,
With a punchline that lands like gravity's trick!

Galactic Glee and Clownish Dreams

Whimsical wonders swirl through the night,
As stardust confetti fills the sky bright.
Jovial beings with laughter to share,
In the great cosmic circus, they float without care.

Eccentric orbs giggle in steadfast play,
While moonbeam jesters brighten the way.
Galaxies twirl with joy in their hearts,
In the vast open space, each humor imparts.

Laughter erupts like a shooting star,
Echoing through the cosmos, near and far.
Puppets of plasma in colorful jest,
Fill our universe with dreams at their best.

Fanciful rhythms of chaotic fun,
With moons in a row, like clowns on the run.
Their talent is boundless, their grins so wide,
In the realm of existence, joy's never dried.

Laughter Lurking in the Nebula

In the misty embrace of a nebula's hug,
Laughter erupts like a gentle tug.
Stars play peek-a-boo in the swirling haze,
While wit's ghostly whispers dance in a blaze.

Jokes tumble forth from the clouds above,
Carried by comets, wrapped in love.
Alien chuckles echo through the void,
In the cosmic mystery, humor deployed.

Planets gossip with cheeky delight,
As supernovas burst in the deep of the night.
Their raucous laughter fills the expanse,
Creating a cosmic circus in a never-ending dance.

Jesters of the cosmos, they twirl and fling,
In the great universe, they celebrate spring.
With playful intent, they tickle the dark,
In every corner, laughter leaves its mark.

Souvenirs from the Cosmic Carnival

In stars stitched with laughter, the clowns jump and play,
With luminous confetti that brightens the way.
Galaxies twirl like balloons in the night,
Whimsical wonders in a pixelated sight.

The planets spin stories, each one a delight,
Riding comets like horses, in graceful flight.
Bright balloons filled with giggles and glee,
Echoing laughter from the cosmic marquee.

Gravity's grip is a rubbery thing,
As space jesters somersault, cartwheel, and swing.
An alien band plays a merry old tune,
Under the watch of a disco-lit moon.

With every twinkle, a joke floats on by,
In this carnival limitless, up in the sky.
Souvenirs of joy, like stars, we will keep,
In the heart of the universe, where dreams never sleep.

Jokin' with Jupiter

Under the great swirling clouds of deep hues,
Jovial jesters trade celestial views.
With rings made of laughter and moons made of cheer,
They tickle the atmosphere, spreading good cheer.

Jupiter chuckles with thunderous delight,
As comets perform in a dance of pure light.
The gasbags float by with jokes to incite,
While Saturn spins tales of whimsical fright.

A wink of a star, a flip of a flare,
Cosmic pranks bounce like bubbles in air.
Through the jests and the jives, the laughter soars high,
In the court of great giants, the chuckles won't die.

With every jovial giggle, a planet spins round,
In the joken' embrace where true fun can be found.
No frown can endure in this jester's domain,
As humor erupts like a meteor's rain.

Quirky Quasars and Tales

Through the cosmic expanse where the bright eat their cake,
Quasars sparkle and shimmer, while space jesters shake.
With punchlines that echo in darkness untold,
They twist every atom into humor so bold.

A tail of a comet spins tales of delight,
Full of quirky surprises that dance in the night.
Each quasar's a beacon, a ticklish tease,
As they wink at the void with comedic ease.

With space-time unfurling like ribbons so bright,
The humor is endless, a buoyant sight.
Each story a burst of illumination's spark,
Lighting up hearts in the deep cosmic dark.

So let's laugh with the stars, and giggle with glee,
Share the humor of infinity, wild and free.
In this grand universe, we'll make our own fate,
With quirky quasars and tales to create.

Astral Antics in a Celestial Playground

In the playground of planets where nonsense must reign,
Swing sets of stardust and slides made of rain.
Frolicking moons choke on giggly delight,
While shooting stars play tag, a marvelous sight.

Each galaxy tumbles with pranks full of flair,
Laughter explodes like fireworks in the air.
Around every corner, a joke takes its flight,
As gravity giggles and dims the starlight.

Teeter-totters wobble, with playful intent,
While pulsars sputter jokes that leave us content.
An audience gathered in cosmic embrace,
For the antics abound in this whimsical space.

So let's join the laughter, abandon the frown,
In this astral playground, we'll dance 'round and 'round.
With each gleam and chuckle, let joy be unfurled,
In the heart of the heavens, let laughter be twirled.

Cosmic Cabaret of the Comets

In the velvet sky, stars wear their hats,
Juggling planets, bouncing like acrobats.
Galaxies waltz in goofy line dance,
With twinkling giggles, they all take a chance.

Meteor showers pour like confetti bright,
As comets skate through the velvet night.
The moon plays piano, a cheerful refrain,
While asteroids cheer, creating a chain.

A dance-off erupts, all cosmic and wild,
With Saturn's rings hosting, oh so beguiled.
Stars sharing secrets, with laughter they share,
In this cosmic cabaret, joy fills the air.

Stardust Shenanigans

In a galaxy far, where the giggles abound,
Stardust mischief twirls round and round.
Supernova's sparkle, a dazzling prank,
As quarks make faces, in quantum hijinks, they clank.

Asteroids race, a raucous parade,
While black holes chuckle at the games they've played.
Twinkling stars flick, like clever jesters,
In this stardust circus, all are investors.

Constellations conspire, a secretive plot,
To tickle the sun, oh, it matters a lot!
Comets fly by with a wink and a grin,
In this world of wonders, let laughter begin!

The Nebula's Nonsensical Ball

In a vibrant nebula, colors collide,
Where laughs echo wide, and glee cannot hide.
Planets wearing masks for a grand masquerade,
As starlight cascades in a joyful parade.

Bubbles of gas swirl in syncopated beats,
While the universe grooves on its myriad seats.
Dancing through space with rhythm divine,
Aliens tapping their little toe's line.

Black holes do the limbo, they bend and they sway,
While quasars shout out, "Have fun, come and play!"
A riot of colors, a sight to behold,
In this nonsensical ball, laughter unfolds!

A Universe Wrapped in Laughter

A universe wrapped in giggles and cheer,
Satellites spinning, their joy we can hear.
Galactic balloons float in the breeze,
While laughter erupts with whimsical ease.

Pulsars blinking in a playful delight,
While starships zoom past in a comical flight.
Every quasar gleams with a cheeky spark,
As they dance on the edge of the dark.

In this cosmic haven, silliness reigns,
Wormholes chuckle, creating new lanes.
A cosmos where smiles light up the night,
Boundless joy weaves through the starlit sight.